How to Obtain Sponsorship for your Race Team

Table of Contents

Preface

Racing is expensive. When I first started racing, I read, unless you can afford to go to the bank, withdraw $10,000, and throw hundred dollar bills out the window on the way home, then you can't afford it, just forget about it. That would be true if you plan to pay for this completely out of your pocket. However, unless you are rich and throwing money away is no object, you will need sponsorship to maintain your hobby, especially if you plan to be competitive. Have you ever seen a Nascar team roll out onto the track without a sponsor? Some of these team owners are uber rich, and still, they are not throwing their money out the window, their sponsors are footing the bill.

If you are reading this, you are either; considering buying a racecar and are seeking the knowledge of how to obtain sponsorship to help pay for the cost; you have recently purchased a racecar and are now trying to figure out

Preface

how you could possibly financially maintain this hobby; or you have been racing for a while and are getting close to expiring your available funding for this adrenaline pumping sport. No matter which category you fall into, if you read this book and are willing to put in the effort, you WILL land sponsorship.

In the following chapters I will outline my very own PROVEN methods of success in finding sponsorship. On the race track, I have minimal experience, (30) races as of this writing; I have demonstrated very lack luster talent behind the wheel, but I have garnered sponsorship from multiple companies, and not just mom-n-pop's grocery store down on the corner, or uncle Joe's farm.

What is Sponsorship?

Hmm... Let's break this into two parts, what sponsor ship is not and then build back up to what sponsorship is.

First of all, I have used the word "sponsorship" up until this point, only because it is the term you are probably most familiar with. However, this term has been rode hard and put up wet. It has been overused and abused by the majority of grass roots racecar drivers. The term is more appropriately used in regard to your son's rec league baseball team. When a rec league baseball team ask for sponsorship, they are asking for money that will be used to help the kids. That money will help pay for uniforms, referees, equipment, etc. The "sponsor" is willing to do this because they are giving back to the community and it helps build their reputation, within the community, as a company that cares about the kids. Advertising or marketing is not a direct part of this strategy.

What is Sponsorship?

The terms "Sponsor" and "Sponsorship" have developed a negative connotation, and using them with your potential "sponsors" is very likely to prevent them from "sponsoring" you. Here is how it comes across to most people:

What you said: "Would you like to sponsor my racecar?"
What they heard: "I have spent all my money on my racecar, and was wondering if you would like to provide me with a handout so that I can continue."

Really? This doesn't sound much different than your Meth addicted cousin Earl asking you to borrow $200 so he can buy groceries to feed his 5 kids. Earl is still strung out from his latest binge, got fired from his job yesterday and you know you aren't getting that money back, but at least Earl has your empathy for those children. When you own a racecar, you have lost all hope for financial empathy from anyone, ever.

What is Sponsorship?

So, forget the words "Sponsor" and "Sponsorship." Remove them from your vocabulary, forever. Never say them in public again. From this point forward, replace those words with Marketing Partner or Marketing Partnership. Not only does this sound much more professional, but it is used so rarely, that most people will have to stop and think about what that means. Let these words paint a picture for them of what you are asking. You are now asking them to partner with you to market their products or services. Now, you have the little car in their mind up on the bars, hooked up and turning left.

Legal Preparation

I know, you were just getting into this, starting to anticipate what I would say next, and maybe even thinking of how you could be someone's marketing partner. But, you were told in the drivers meeting not to jump the start or you would be rolled back a spot. So, here is the caution flag for jumping the start. Now, let's restart.

If you want to do this right, and I mean RIGHT, there are some things you need to get done before approaching anyone for a Marketing Partnership. First, you need to go to your local County Courthouse and obtain a business license. The cost of this will vary depending on where you live, but you will likely find that this business license will only cost you $15 to $30. You will be allowed to operate under just your social security number until you reach some profit limit that your county will impose. In my area that number is $10,000. Meaning, until my business produces $10,000 or more in PROFIT, I do not need a tax ID number. However, you still must keep good records of your expenses and revenue.

Legal Preparation

You WILL need to report your profit/loss at tax time. Most likely, until you get really, really good at this marketing partnership pitch, you will have a loss to report and will be able to use that as a deduction on your taxes. WHAT? Yes, that is right, Uncle Sam will be your first sponsor. Yes, this is legal. You are running a business, providing a service to other legal businesses, those businesses will want to claim any money they spend with you as an advertising expense, and so you will need to claim it as income. If your expenses exceed your income you will have a loss. That loss will save you money on your taxes. No, that is not the long-term goal, but the vast majority of businesses in America lose money the first 3-5 years they are in business. I would advise you to obtain a CPA to do your taxes. A good CPA will know what expenses you can claim, equipment you can depreciate, mileage you can claim, etc. On top of these tax benefits, a potential Marketing Partner will be much more receptive to the idea of signing a contract with and writing a check to a licensed business, than they will be to writing a check to "Earl."

Legal Preparation

That leads us to one other legal consideration, a contract. You should create a contract that concisely outlines and itemizes the services you will provide to your partner, as well as what they will pay you for them, how they will pay you for them, and when they will pay you for them. You should define exactly how long your services will be provided, like "one calendar year from the date of signing of this contract." The importance of this contract is just to prevent any misunderstandings and to be sure that both parties are legally bound to the agreement. If it isn't in writing, someone will end up feeling cheated. Put it in writing, no exceptions.

The Marketing Partnership Proposal

Alright! Everyone is lined back up, the light is out, and we are going green out of 4 this time.

There are a plethora of resources available to you online, to aid in writing a great proposal. With that said, I will not delve too deeply into formatting or a writing a proposal. We will simply discuss, from a higher level view, what a Marketing Partnership Proposal is, general ideas for content, and why it is a necessity.

For this Marketing Partnership search to be successful, you will need a Marketing Partnership Proposal. This isn't hard, but, like anything in life, the more preparation you put in, the more success you will have. So, lets brainstorm.

Start thinking of all the things you could do, that would actually help someone to sell more of their products or services. You will need to get your mind out of the box and start thinking out here where the money is, outside the box. Hint, a sticker on your racecar isn't going to get it done.

The Marketing Partnership Proposal

Telling them how you won 32 races last year isn't going to sell anything for them, (unless, your target partner is a chassis builder or engine builder, MAYBE.)

Maybe you are good with video editing and could provide them a high quality commercial that could be televised. Maybe, you have 4 million YouTube viewers and you could advertise their products or services there. Maybe, you have a ton of personal contacts that use products or services similar to theirs and you can influence them to change over. Maybe you have thousands of followers on Facebook, Linked In, Snap Chat, Instagram, or Twitter. Maybe you know someone who is an influencer in a specific market and can pay them to help you advertise for your partner. These are SERVICES you can provide, and are a much more valuable asset than any passive advertising. None of these services are dependent on your level of racing talent.

The Marketing Partnership Proposal

You have a racecar, and probably an enclosed trailer. This is passive advertising space that can be decorated with wraps and decals. I bet you have T-shirts printed every year, you could include their logos on those. You could also offer them T-shirts, hats, coffee mugs, ink pens, or business cards, with or without any mention of your racecar on them. What? You don't have the resources to provide these things? I will pretend I didn't hear that thought. YES, you do. Jim Bob's T-shirt shop down on main-street will make any T-shirt you want. Kinkos across the street will print any business card you want. Yes, the potential Marketing Partner could go directly to Kinkos or Jim Bobs, OR, maybe you could figure out what the partner wants on a T-shirt or business card, and you could go get it done for him. Now, you are offering another service to go along with this passive advertising. Don't let lack of equipment or resources prevent you from offering whatever service you dream up. You CAN get it done.

The Marketing Partnership Proposal

Now, you have brainstormed for 3 weeks and you have a ton of ideas that you think offer some value to your potential partner. It is time to figure out what these ideas will cost you. For example, you want to offer "25 T-shirts" as part of one of your service packages. So, you need to know how much Jim Bob is going to charge you for 25 T-shirts. Call Bob and find out. Ok, Bob has a 25 pc minimum at $12 each. Now you know it will cost you $300 to provide those T-shirts. As a very general rule, I would suggest that you at least double all of your cost for products like this. But, I would not itemize them within your proposal. Instead, I would suggest providing an overview of all services and products you are offering in the package and assign a single price for the package.

- Gold Package ($7500)
  - Weekly advertising on all our social media accounts
  - 10" x 24" decal on each rear quarter panel of racecar
  - 48" x 48" decal on back door of enclosed trailer

The Marketing Partnership Proposal

- o 25 T-shirts with your logo on the front and our race team design on back

In this example, you need to know what those decals or wraps will cost you to have made and installed, how much those T-shirts will cost you, how much you value the time that you will spend advertising on social media, how much time that high quality video commercial will cost, what it will cost to have it aired on TV, what it will cost to print business cards for the partner. Now, your **price** point (to the partner) needs to cover all of that **cost**, PLUS provide you with some cash to keep that racecar running. Do not neglect your time in this equation. Do you want to work for free? Are you willing to work for $5/hour? $10, $20, $50? A $7500 "sponsorship" may sound like a lot, and it would be if it were that original handout that you and Earl were asking for, but now, you have an expense to provide these services. So, you might only get $4500 of that to put toward the racecar.

The Marketing Partnership Proposal

How much time did you invest? 100 hours, then you made $45/hour. 300 hours? Then you made $15/hr. See the picture? Your time is valuable, and you only have 24 hours per day just like everyone else. Get paid for your time.

Finding your Target Marketing Partner

To find a marketing partner that you can really offer value to, you will need to spend some time thinking about the products and services that you are or can be most passionate about. You will essentially be a salesman for them that will not get a weekly paycheck. If you expect them to partner with you again next year, you will need to demonstrate that you can make them more money. I'm betting that you will not be very efficient at selling makeup for your wife's friend. But, you could probably sell helmets, or car wraps, or do a great job of promoting Jim Bob's T-shirt shop as the best around. You will have more fun and be more successful with this if you choose a product or service that you can really stand behind.

Connecting with Potential Marketing Partners

You will likely find that Jim Bob doesn't have a marketing budget and Mary Kay isn't interested in advertising with you, and mom-n-pops grocery store "sponsored" someone last year and didn't really get anything out of it. (More than likely because XYZ Racing was only looking for a handout, they took mom-n-pops money, threw their logo on the car and were done.) Maybe you can overcome some of that and persuade a previously burned "sponsor" to give you an opportunity to make them money. You will need to expand your search and really open your mind up to more products and services that you can stand behind.

I have found Linked In to be a great resource when searching for potential partners. You can basically search for people by job title, "marketing director," or "Owner," or "business development manager." You need to make contact with the people that have the authority to say yes to your proposal.

Connecting with Potential Marketing Partners

Anyone can say no. Send as many friend invites as you can, to significant figures.

Two rules of advertising will apply here also, (1) target market, don't waste your time or contact limits adding bank managers or real estate brokers. (Facebook only allows you 5,000 friends, choose them wisely) (2) This is a numbers game, and you will realize that less than 1% of the people you reach out to will result in a Partnership. This means you will probably have to reach out to 200 or more people just to gain a single Partner. What? You need 5 partners? Oh, well, simple math tells you that you will have to reach out to over 1,000 people to get 5 partners. I can attest to this fact in my own Partnership searches.

Wow, that seems like a lot of work. IT IS WORK. If you are willing to WORK, you can get paid. If you are not willing to work, you are back to wanting a handout. Damn Earl, you got to get it together. No one wants to pay for you to ride around in a racecar.

Connecting with Potential Marketing Partners

Most of the people who do welcome you to send your proposal will likely not get back to you and you will become discouraged. It is your job to follow up if you want an answer. Don't push too hard, but DO make them say no if they don't want to do it, DO NOT let them leave you hanging. If they keep telling you to check back later, then keep checking back later. You will acquire most of your partners during this stage. In fact, it may even be a test to grade your follow up skills. I mean, when you start trying to help sell their products or services to others, you will very likely have to play the follow up game. If you can't follow up to further your own business, why would they trust that you would follow up to sell their products or services? You must follow up, probably more than once, maybe more than 10-12 times.

Closing the Deal

To me, this is the fun part. However, with any negotiation, both parties normally compromise and each get less than they were aiming for. You should anticipate some of this on the front end. What I mean by that is, when you build your proposal do not set your price points at your bottom dollar price, leave yourself room to negotiate.

Also, when you build your proposal, it may end up being very vanilla and somewhat of a cookie cutter format. You will offer the "Gold Package," "Silver Package," and the "Bronze Package." I will fill you in on a secret now, you have a low chance of ever selling one of these packages in the exact terms that you lay it out. So, be ready to negotiate and be open to various forms of Partnership.

The partner may prefer to make you a dealer and allow you to sell their products and make a commission. This is really the best solution for them, because they don't pay you anything unless you are performing and making them money. This option is also good for you because it has very little cost, except your time.

Closing the Deal

Another possibility is simply that they offer their services to you at a reduced cost. Don't turn your nose up at this offer. I once worked a deal with my real estate agent to reduce his commission by 2% when he sold my home. This saved me $4,200. On another partnership, I bartered my marketing services in exchange for 50 T-shirts with my racing design and 50 hats with my number on them. I was able to sell these and produce nearly $2,000 in racing funds.

There will be times when you are just about to have your new wrap installed, but you don't have all of your available space sold. You might offer a spot on your car to someone for a few hundred bucks. This isn't a big time sponsorship, but it is a few hundred that you didn't and wouldn't have if you didn't make the deal. Most likely this will only be a decal on your car, and not the full blown marketing package that you are offering larger partners.

Use Caution Before Accepting any Deal

My first major Marketing Partner was SolidCam Inc. I am telling you, there are no words to describe how ecstatic I was to be on the telephone with these guys discussing a partnership. They could have offered anything and I probably would have accepted it, then. They weren't interested in any of my cookie cutter packages. They made me an offer that was basically take it or leave it. The offer was:

- $3,000 cash
- A yearly renewable licensed copy of their software (SolidCam and an OEM SolidWorks)
- To enroll me in their "Business Alliance Partner" program.
  - Under this program, I would have the opportunity to generate a nice commission off any referral I provided that led to a sale.

Use Caution Before Accepting any Deal

That was the offer they provided in return for the following:

- 60 sq ft decal on each side of my racecar trailer
- 2 sq ft logo on each side of my car
- Attend an open house with them at a local CNC machine retailer
- And try to round up as many referrals as possible.

Does this sound like a good deal to you? I thought so, and jumped on it without much consideration. I almost, and very easily could have, lost my A$$. But, I had already accepted their money and signed a contract, there was no turning back at this point. The first quote I received for those trailer decals was $3500, installed. I shopped around and got them much cheaper, but I had to put them on myself. This was very tedious and time consuming and required the help of 2 other people. Fortunately, these were family members who volunteered. But, wasn't there time valuable too?

Use Caution Before Accepting any Deal

The open house event I agreed to, was a two day event, in the middle of the week. I had to take time off from my real job to go do this. I had vacation time and was able to schedule it, but, shouldn't that at least have been worth the money that I was losing by not being at my job?

You just need to be mindful of every single aspect of any deal you make, be sure you know all of the cost and be sure you are making money. If you wanted to lose money there are much easier ways than putting in all of this effort.

Activation

Great! You are a licensed business, you have a Marketing Partnership Proposal, you have emailed, called, or knocked on 10,000 doors, and you have all of your contracts signed, and have cashed a few checks. Now, If you have any intention of retaining these Marketing Partners for next year, you better get to work and uphold your end of the bargain. You have a legal binding contract to fulfill and could potentially be sued if you fail to deliver everything you said you would deliver.

If you offered hospitality events, you need to get these scheduled as soon as possible, and begin making plans. I prefer to do these before the racing season actually begins, because, as you know, there is no guarantee you will even have a racecar after your next visit to the racetrack. When the lean, mean, money consuming machine hits the track it is at risk to be completely destroyed. Have some integrity and remember that the commitments you made in exchange for hundreds or thousands of someone's hard earned money are more important than you actually racing.

Activation

If you agreed to work for a commission, you don't really have any commitments to uphold, but if you want to make any money from those deals, then you need to schedule time out of your life to push their products or services. There are many ways to do this, but social media marketing is the easiest way in my opinion. Again, you will find this to be a numbers game. You need to choose 4850 of your Facebook friends to be people that will buy the products you are trying to sell.

Two of my Marketing Partners are PITBULL Lifts and Velocita Premium Motorsports Apparel. So, I have added nearly 5,000 dirt track racers across the country to my friends list, and have joined over 100 groups related to dirt track racing. I have experienced some decent success with selling both product groups to this target audience.

If your wife's friend did sponsor you with a makeup company, then you might consider adding 4850 women, ages 35-65, as this will be the target market for you, not dirt track racers.